Contents

Time *for* Me

Self-Care and Simple Pleasures for Women Who Do Too Much

HELENE LERNER

simple **truths**
▶ Small books. BIG IMPACT.

Note this is a new edition of a work
from 2015. Names, dates, and
roles have not been updated.

Originally published as *Time for Me* in 2015 in the United States of America by
Sourcebooks. This edition issued based on the hardcover edition published in 2015
in the United States of America by Simple Truths, an imprint of Sourcebooks.

Published by Simple Truths, an imprint of Sourcebooks
P.O. Box 4410, Naperville, Illinois 60567-4410
(630) 961-3900
sourcebooks.com

Printed and bound in the United States of America.
VP 10 9 8 7 6 5 4 3 2 1

Introduction

Do you relate to any of these?

- You get up in the morning, and no matter how much sleep you've had, you're still tired.
- You look in the mirror and your eyes seem dull and without sparkle.
- You get ready to go to work and your routine seems mechanical. You feel as if you could do your tasks blindfolded.
- Although you like your job and consider yourself powerful, you lack the enthusiasm you once had.

If you answered yes to two or more of these statements, you are probably one of the "me-time" weary. It's so easy to get distracted doing important things for everyone else and forget about what we need. A woman's basic needs include: food, clothing, shelter, passion, friendship, and *fun*!

Yes, fun. The original and most potent form of self-care. It lightens our burden, gives us new perspectives, and frees our minds to face challenging situations, knowing that we can handle anything that comes along. **Fun reduces the feeling that you're being drained by the stressors of life.** It gives you a greater sense of contentment.

This book contains simple ways to nourish your spirit—I call them simple pleasures. By introducing moments of fun and enjoyment into your life, you'll be able to reignite your passion and energy day in and day out. Plus, caring for yourself as you care for others is just a good practice.

Don't you deserve to treat yourself with the kindness and care you give to others? **Yes, you do.**

Here's the good news: at any point in time, we can wake up to what we need. If we are stretched and drained, we can change that. If we are irritable because we've said yes too many times—when in our heart of hearts we really meant no—it's possible to communicate differently. In fact, when we do, we become even more powerful because we are prioritizing *our* choices.

Awareness is the first step, then summoning the courage to do things differently, even if that doesn't feel comfortable. **Change happens when we allow ourselves to go through—and grow through—discomfort.**

But, you might ask, what will happen to the responsibilities I "should" be taking care of? What about the work that I "should" be finishing? I am here to tell you that nothing will happen, except that you will flourish.

You may have to give up some things as you put your own self-care first, like guilt, worry, people-pleasing, and perfectionism. But that's a small price to pay for contentment and satisfaction…isn't it?

In this book, I will offer a program for carving out more personal time, based on my work with thousands of women who are influential but also spread themselves too thin. It consists of four Power Keys to a more joyful and balanced life—Clarity, Letting Go, Pleasure, and Practice.

Interspersed throughout the book are "Me-Time Victors," diverse women who made a shift and no longer put their self-care needs last on their to-do lists. Their personal time is as important to them as the time they spend on family, career, and community activities. These women will offer insights and practical tips, and it is my hope that you will make some of their practices your own.

Try our suggestions. What have you got to lose except dark shadows under your eyes, a lackluster feeling, and living life in one dull, stressed out color—gray?

You have everything to gain—sparkle, energy, and enthusiasm. And you'll have access to all Twelve Powers of a Woman—read on to learn more.

Know this truth: **at this very moment, you are enough, just the way you are.**

Not having enough time is something most of us deal with.

However, look more closely. Are you filling yourself up with endless activity because underneath you feel like you are not enough—that what you do and have falls short of some imaginary standard that you can *never* reach?

We need to challenge these feelings of lack and counter them by speaking the truth. Take on a new mantra: *I have enough, I do enough, and I AM enough.*

If we don't believe this, we can act as if it's true. As we exchange old thoughts for new ones, we develop self-mastery and gain access to a woman's Twelve Powers:

1. **The Power of Imperfection.** This power gives us the ability to show up for life and allows us to be messy. Great learning happens when we admit we don't have all the answers and can risk making mistakes.

2. **The Power of Handling Discomfort.** To let go of habits we've outgrown and move on, we must summon the courage to explore new territory, and that doesn't feel comfortable.

3. **The Power of Authenticity.** Many of us were brought up to be "nice" and not create waves. When we trust intuition and say what we feel, we are truly ourselves.

4. **The Power of Discipline.** Contrary to the common point of view, having a disciplined lifestyle creates order and freedom.

5. **The Power of Kindness.** We need to treat ourselves as we do others, to practice self-love by being nonjudgmental and nurturing.

6. **The Power of Acknowledgment.** False modesty is inauthentic; we have many talents and abilities that are ours to claim.

7. **The Power of Receiving.** Most of us are givers, but receiving is just as important—opening ourselves up to the generosity of others.

8. **The Power of Letting Go.** Destructive habits die hard, and to lead a more fulfilling life, we must give them up.

9. **The Power of Trust.** When we have faith to move forward despite uncertainty, we experience life's greatness.

10. **The Power of Courage.** Dare to live fully. Dare to dream and think bigger. With courage, we can do that.

11. **The Power of Risk.** We must move out of our comfort zones. It gets easier as we take one right action at a time.

12. **The Power of Intuition.** There's an inner knowing we all have; we just need to quiet our minds and listen to it.

The Time for Me Program

It's an easy program for complicated people, consisting of four power keys.

Power Key No. 1—Clarity

In part one, you will learn more about why you are not as fulfilled as you would like to be, and you will be encouraged to take risks to change this.

Power Key No. 2—Letting Go

Part two will help you say no to ways of acting that do not serve you and yes to what does. For example, you may find it difficult to turn down someone's request and feel guilty when you do. You'll become aware of impediments that keep you stuck and learn the tools to move on.

Power Key No. 3—Pleasure

In part three, you will uncover and explore your passions—committing to activities that have the sole purpose of pleasing you. (Yes, you are entitled to that, and you're not being selfish!)

Power Key No. 4—Practice

Finally, part four offers daily reflections and exercises that will enable you to flex your inner muscles. I'll ask you to put insights from this book into practice.

As you start the program, you will undoubtedly feel some fear. Why shouldn't you? You are in uncharted territory. Change feels uncomfortable. But don't let that distract you. This type of discomfort confirms that you are growing.

Just continue and keep focused on your goal: to lead a more joyful and fulfilling life.

It's your life, and it only happens once. Why not make it a great one?

What are you hoping to gain by following our program? What are your most important goals?

Power Key No. 1

Clarity

Awareness is the first step toward changing. Reflect on the following questions: On the work front, which of your daily tasks feel mechanical and routine? What dreams have you put on hold because your day-to-day responsibilities take priority? What do you believe is possible or impossible for you to achieve?

If money were not a concern, how would you spend your time— what career or activities would you actively be involved in?

....

....

....

....

Time Bandits

What "robs" you of time? Do you feel guilty about taking time for yourself? Do you have difficulty saying "no" when someone asks for help? In general, do you judge yourself harshly? Know that it's possible to change and take on new ways of behaving, but it will require you to step outside your comfort zone.

JEAN MESSNER

Artist, administrator, divorced mother of a teenage son

In 2009, I was laid off from my job of nineteen years as a legal secretary. I was fifty-eight years old and looking for work, competing with college grads. Ageism was prevalent. I was panicked and felt hopeless, and my savings were dwindling. I got through that time by allowing myself to create art; it's my passion.

I reached out to a successful artist who became my mentor, and I started painting every day—it lifted my spirits. He encouraged me to show my work. I started in my apartment and then had a painting exhibited in a restaurant, then a gallery, a museum, and a large convention center. Later, I was able to get a full-time job as an administrator, which provides financial support for my art.

Time Bandit

It's hard to come home after work and feel creative. However, if I put the paints and canvas out in my workspace, I find that I'm drawn to doing it. If I don't paint at night, then I usually wake up early in the morning and paint before work.

Time Enhancers

- Pay attention to your body—know when it needs to be replenished.
- Get a self-care buddy and check in with each other.
- With no guilt, take a nap, whenever possible!

Jean's Simple Pleasures

- painting, of course
- visiting a museum
- watching an old movie
- cooking a meal for myself and serving it on nice china
- browsing an art gallery

Jean's Best Advice

Plan your day and schedule time to do what makes you feel good.

On the Power of Discipline

I need structure and order to be free. When I make a commitment that no matter what I will paint for an hour, either in the evening or before work in the morning, I do it! My word is my bond.

On the Power of Trust

I don't know how I will earn my living from my art, but I take small actions to make it happen, and my career is growing. I have lots of support from people who believe in me when I get discouraged.

What are some simple activities that make you feel good? List as many as you can and then pick a few that you can start including in your week, if not your day-to-day.

As you proceed through the program, take risks and try new things. Take action toward achieving goals that you may not feel able to reach. Go for it! If fear surfaces, let it. Realize there is no guarantee that something negative won't happen, even during routine activities. So you might as well take a chance on something that can transform your life.

After you keep doing what you thought was risky, it becomes easier to take more risks. Think of your first day at your current job or how you felt when you found out you were going to be a mom—all these changes involved risk, but you did them. Now, going to work and taking care of the kids seem so natural. When you step out in a new direction, you're bound to feel uncomfortable. It's important to honor this discomfort because it means you are changing. In fact, if you keep pressing on, you may find that your fear turns into excitement.

Dream bigger,

Think bigger...

You are more capable than you know.

What are some risks you can start taking right now, today? If they pan out, how can they change your future for the better?

Letting Go

Part two will help you shed habits you may have outgrown but are afraid to let go of, like perfectionism, not being able to say "no," an oversensitivity toward criticism, and procrastination. Discarding them will not be easy because you've probably been acting that way for a long time. But with the tools you'll learn here, you can start to take more nurturing actions for yourself.

As you begin, you're bound to make mistakes along the way. Don't get discouraged. Instead, keep moving forward as if your new mindset is one you've had for a while. Remind yourself that your goal is to be more self-nurturing and to increase the joyful moments in your life. Like physical exercise, building muscles (in this case, "inner" muscles) involves growing pains, which will lessen the more you practice.

We are so used to feeling under pressure that we believe stress is a normal part of everyday life. But the truth is, we are stressed because we are "stressable." It's not the situations in our lives that cause us stress but our reactions to them.

Write down your biggest stressors during the day. How do you usually react to each one of them? Then make another list of your stressors and alternative ways of reacting to them.

Try them out the next time you are triggered.

Perfectionism

Are you a perfectionist? Let's try a simple exercise to explore. Think about how you've handled specific situations as you reflect on the questions below.

- Do you set unusually high standards for yourself and others and get disappointed if they are not met?
- Are you rarely satisfied after you have accomplished a task, not giving yourself the credit you deserve?
- Do you lose perspective easily, treating a minor task as importantly as a major one?
- Are you overly sensitive to criticism and dwell on it even after the moment has passed?

If you've said yes to any of these questions—join the club. Perfectionism is usually riddled with the fear that we will be judged harshly if we don't do something the "right" way.

With women's late entry into the workforce, we've had to prove ourselves on the job, often having to be twice as good as our male counterparts. If we don't measure up to this exaggerated standard (who could?), we are made to—or make ourselves—feel inadequate. Let's support each other to stop doing that. We do more than our fair share as it is. **Besides, no one is really keeping score, except us.**

Let go of a negative thought that is pulling you down. Here are some strategies to help you change your perspective and treat yourself more kindly:

- Before you engage in an activity, think positively. Tell yourself you are about to embark on a task that will be completed in a timely and efficient manner, even if it isn't done perfectly.
- When you make a mistake, don't dwell on it. Look at how you could have done things differently and move on. Think to yourself, "Next!"
- Congratulate yourself when you do something out of the ordinary. For example, tell yourself, "Way to go, girl!" when you make time during the week to have dinner with friends.

How are you perfectionistic? Pick one example. What happened? What went wrong? What expectations did you have of yourself? Now, change the channel. Focus on what you did right in this situation.

TRY THIS

Course Correct: If you feel yourself tensing up because your mind is racing with negative thoughts, stop whatever you are doing. Sit quietly and become aware of your body and what you are telling yourself. For example, my mouth is dry; I feel tightness in my throat; I am thinking that my report is not good enough. Now, calm yourself by affirming that what you are doing is more than adequate and that you have the time and energy to complete the task successfully.

Criticism

Criticism, if constant, is as harmful to your well-being as perfectionism. For example, let's say a coworker belittles your performance at a meeting, and suddenly your feelings of inadequacy are triggered. Although you try not to let this bother you, you feel defensive, thinking, "She has no business criticizing me because she's not my supervisor." Her comments most likely stem from her own insecurity and may not be related to what you've done.

The lesson here: take what fits and leave the rest! Your priority is to be gracious toward yourself, to pick up what's constructive and not dwell on what won't help you grow.

TRY THIS

The Practical Pause: The next time someone strikes out at you, breathe deeply and don't react immediately. If it's appropriate to assert yourself, do. Say how you feel, using an "I" statement. For example, "I feel uncomfortable because you brought that up in front of my boss." When you've said what you needed to, let it go. After all, you've judged your fair share of people, too.

When you feel you are about to criticize someone, pause! Examine why you feel agitated. Is it because of what she is doing? Or are you reminded of something that you don't want to face about yourself?

What you think or say about others is a reflection of how you feel about yourself. So, be mindful of your words. They have the power to shape your reality. If you find fault with people, they feel judged. If you are supportive, they're more likely to feel safe and confident.

However, not all criticism is harmful. For example, honest feedback is one of the greatest gifts you can receive because it is given with the intention of helping you grow, so you don't want to push it away.

What criticism is taking up headspace that you need to let go of? How can you either shift it into constructive feedback or let it go?

TRY THIS

Repeat and Reflect: When someone gives you feedback, repeat what's been said and acknowledge that you understand it. Although you may feel defensive, say nothing more. For example, you might say to your boss, "On a whole, you are pleased with my performance, but I've made quite a few mistakes lately on the client's weekly report and I need to proofread my work better." Or to your teenage daughter, "You are angry because I've missed the last two soccer games. And I must go to the one coming up." Repeating a comment gives you the space to reflect on it, before saying something you will regret later on.

The Power of No

Have you ever agreed to do something just because you were afraid of a disapproving reaction if you declined? In other words, you didn't feel entitled to say no. Turning someone down is still a challenge for many of us. We want to please others because we want to be liked. But we simply can't be all things to all people.

Saying no can be positive when it frees you to do what is most beneficial for you and others. Saying yes too many times may mean you want others to like you by trying to be who they want you to be. Have faith that they will like you even better for who you are. And, if they don't, you may need to move on.

How can you get better about saying no? You need to evaluate new requests for your help with the existing commitments you have. Many of us try to find a way to do everything and sacrifice our health and sanity in the process. If you say yes to a request, you most likely will have to let another commitment go and make a choice based upon what seems most important at the moment.

Take this scenario, for example. Someone asks you to assist at the company picnic, which involves helping to plan the event as well as staffing a table that day. Ask yourself, *What will I have to give up in order to do this? Will taking this on better suit my needs?* You may say yes, because it's an opportunity to meet new people and be visible in the department. If you do, you will have to tell a coworker you can't assist with his project any longer. You may want to help him look for a replacement.

Here's another example. Your boss asks you to participate in a meeting that conflicts with your child's piano recital. If you consider the meeting to be relatively unimportant, you've just finished working on a report that required overtime, and you've spent time away from your family, then tell your boss, "I can't be there." However, if the meeting is with the head of the division and it would be important for you to attend, you may decide differently. Grandparents or your significant other can cover for you at the performance, but under no circumstances can you miss the next one.

Likewise, "no" is appropriate if you've just come back from a family vacation, are tired and a little under the weather, and your significant other wants you to go to a movie with friends. If the response you receive is less than enthusiastic, hold your ground—even if you feel a bit guilty or angry when you do.

Each situation demanding your time calls for a unique response. For instance, if you haven't seen each other much lately and your friend wants to spend quality time together, it's important to find a way to do that.

Let's face it: even when we juggle responsibilities, whatever choice we make comes with some degree of guilt. The question is, how do we let it go since it serves no purpose other than making us feel bad? The key is to dismiss a guilty thought as soon as it occurs. **When we pay little attention to guilt, it doesn't have the power to control our actions and, in fact, diminishes.**

How can you say NO to a person who is asking too much of you? Write a script of what you would say and practice it with a trusted friend or in the mirror. Why not give it try? Start writing your script below.

TRY THIS

Practice Makes Perfect: The more you practice saying no, the easier it will get. Think about a situation with a boss, husband, child, or friend that you should have declined but didn't. It could be anything from a dinner invitation to helping out with a project. Now picture yourself doing it differently. How would circumstances have changed if you had said no?

Delegating

Another reason it's difficult to say no is that we want tasks to be done right, meaning *our way*! (There's our perfectionism showing again.) We don't like giving up control. As a result, we spread ourselves too thin. But as we've seen, doing it all yourself doesn't allow you to fully address the important activities—the ones only you can do or want to do.

By delegating, you get the majority of the work done and share the experience with others. At work, try to give away tasks that don't require your minute-to-minute involvement. If you're at home with your children, let them put away the laundry. So what if the towels aren't folded exactly your way? The chore is completed and they feel good about helping.

Now, what happens if you ask someone to help out and he or she doesn't? How do you handle that? Here's a suggestion: *drop the rope.* Just don't do the task, and see what happens. For example, you ask your teenage daughter to clean up her room, and she doesn't. Don't clean it; just close her door and let her live in the mess. Or you've asked your partner to pick up some juice on the way home and he doesn't. He may change his mind when he's thirsty and there's nothing to drink.

If those you ask for help do come around, remember to praise their efforts—even if it wasn't in *your* time frame.

What absolutely needs to be done by YOU? What can you delegate off your list and onto someone else's? Make a list of what you—and only you—need to do, and then a second list of everything you can have others take off your plate.

Procrastination

Once tasks are properly assigned—the ones you will be responsible for and those given to others—the next step is *getting them done*. If we know what we have to do, why do so many of us procrastinate? It goes deeper than just being lazy. Our fear may be surfacing again.

Sometimes we don't complete a task because we are afraid of failing or we don't feel entitled to succeed. For instance, you put off a job search because inwardly you believe you're not worthy of having a better position—or on the flip side, you may be fearful that you will actually succeed at the task, which brings with it a whole new set of challenges.

A way to tackle procrastination is to prepare for the task at hand. This sets the groundwork for getting the job done. For example, if you need to update your résumé, make a list of your latest accomplishments, write a rough draft, ask a friend to review it, and then proofread one last time.

Waiting until the last minute to undertake projects forces you to maintain an unhealthy crash-and-burn working style. You pay a steep price for this—namely, *your sanity*. **Remember, you can be afraid and take action anyway.**

Here are some strategies to help you move forward:

- When confronted by a task that seems overwhelming, break it down into several actionable steps with a timetable of when you will perform them. It's far easier to tackle small tasks and move one step at a time than make a to-do list of bigger goals that feel like leaps.

- As you achieve each action, acknowledge what you've done. This may seem insignificant, but it isn't. It will give you momentum to do more.
- Set up a simple reward system for when you complete each action. Do something nice for yourself—take a walk, call a friend, etc.

*What is a big goal or task that you've been procrastinating on? What's **really** going on? Write down a fear that is coming up.*

Then break down the goal into simple actions with a timetable of when you will do them.

Get to work! Do one, then another and another.

Petty Grievances

It's easy to get caught up in these situations: a loved one speaking in a harsh tone, a child making his twentieth demand of the hour, a friend overlooking a special invitation, a boss in a grumpy mood. When these things come up (and they always do), they can either continue to irritate us or we can take action to let people know how we feel (if appropriate) and then move on. If we focus on how others have "wronged" us and exaggerate their behavior, we are wasting precious energy that can be put to better use. The choice is ours.

Next time something happens that irritates you and you are holding on to it, ask yourself: *How important is the incident compared to what I truly value? Isn't it more important to have satisfying relationships with family and friends than to dwell on minor irritations?* Enjoy where you are right now!

TRY THIS

The Sixty-Second Inventory. Use this sixty-second inventory during the day. It can help you identify how you are feeling and irritations that may be bothering you. Here's what you do—pause several times during the day for a reality check, and ask yourself:

What am I feeling?

Actually pinpoint the feeling, such as being angry with your boss for not acknowledging the overtime hours you've put in lately or being jealous of a friend who always seems to carve out time for a vacation when you can't. If you have trouble identifying your feelings, call a friend and share what's happening. They may be able to help.

How am I holding on?

You've identified what's bothering you, and maybe it's appropriate to take an action, like telling your friend, "I'm disappointed that you forgot about my dinner party." But once you do this, let it go. Look at the consequences if you don't—it drains your energy so that you can't create what you truly want for yourself.

What am I grateful for in this moment?

To complete the letting-go process, reflect on what you have to be grateful for right now. If you can't think of anything, reflect on the things that you take for granted, such as a roof over your head or food in your refrigerator. Act as if there are a lot of things. (You know what will happen? That will become true for you.)

The process of forgiving empowers us. As we forgive others, we become freer and more effective because we are not living in response to past injuries or injustices; we are choosing who we want to be in the present.

BRANDI HARVEY

Nonprofit leader, sister, girlfriend, mentor, vegan, and stylish world-changer

When you work with people and champion their well-being, you have moments when you feel overwhelmed. I am the executive director of the Steve Harvey Foundation, and we run mentoring camps for boys from single-parent households. Prepping and planning for our families always takes a lot out of me. Usually, I'm left feeling exhausted. When we host our camps, the workdays are eighteen hours long. I feel like I am carrying the world on my shoulders; I want to scream and cry, all at the same time. But you don't, because people are depending on you. I have learned to make time each day *to be by myself.*

Quiet time alone allows me to center myself and focus on the important goals that day. It also gives me the opportunity to pray and read something inspirational. As a former fitness competitor, I learned that the body reacts to the nourishment or malnourishment of our spirit.

Time Bandit

Sometimes, I get in a serious work mode and will not move from my desk all day. I eat there and only take bathroom breaks. Now, I try my best to step out and get some fresh air and sunlight. I am a true believer in the power of vitamin D released through sunshine!

Time Enhancers

- Unplug the tablets, phones, pads, and pods and enjoy life. Be in the moment.
- Set a recurring spa appointment; feeling pampered changes your mood.
- Step out into God's creation—look at the colors of the leaves, flowers, and people. Your creativity will begin to flow.

Brandi's Simple Pleasures

- trying different restaurants with my best friend, my sister Karli
- traveling—meeting new people, seeing other cultures
- reading

Brandi's Best Advice

Listen to your spirit, heart, and body. **Trust your gut more.** Learn to say no when things do not feel right or you don't want to do something.

Rejuvenate, restore, and **renew** are three words to live by. Rejuvenate your spirit through love and laughter. Restore your body through rest. Renew your mind through prayer and forgiveness.

On the Power of Letting Go

For so long, I held on to things that traumatized me in my childhood, and it was crippling my growth. My relationships were stagnant and my mind was paralyzed, all because I was focusing on something that happened twenty years ago. **I made a decision to forgive those who hurt me and then I forgave myself for my personal entrapment.** By doing so, I have received far more than I ever lost.

What are you holding on to that you need to forgive someone, or yourself, for? Write a letter below to that person or to yourself from a deep, heartfelt place.

Power Key No. 3

Pleasure

Now that you have looked at habits that don't serve you and have the tools to let them go, you are ready to take action to bring more pleasure into your life. Part three focuses on your spiritual renewal—taking time for yourself. Let's start by exploring the nature of play.

As children, we create ways of having fun all the time. Unfortunately, as adults, many of us lose our ability to play. We feel overly responsible for others, relegating our "playtime" to the back burner. And we wonder why our lives feel mechanical and uninteresting!

Do you PLAY ENOUGH? When was the last time you felt recharged because you had fun? Write down what you did and who was with you. As a child, what were at least five things you did alone or with friends that were truly fun?

BE GENEROUS TO YOURSELF.

Everyday Pleasures

To have fun and recharge, you don't have to go away for a long weekend or take time off from work. All you need is a little time each day to reconnect with the things that make you joyful. **Give yourself the gift of time. Take an hour a day that is just for you.**

If you've lost touch with these simple pleasures, keep tabs on activities you look forward to, like calling a friend for no reason, splurging on a special dessert, taking a break to step outside, or picking up a book you think you'll never have time to read—and actually starting it.

Need some help coming up with things? The list below contains everyday pleasures from a survey of working women that we conducted for this book:

- Write to a friend you've lost contact with.
- Laugh with your child and allow yourself to be silly.
- Take quiet time. Sit in a comfortable chair for at least five to ten minutes.
- Give yourself a foot massage.
- Practice mindfulness. Take a walk and be open to all five senses.
- Visit a jazz bar and enjoy the music and ambience.
- Run bathwater and put some aromatic oils in it, then luxuriate.
- Read a chapter from a "juicy" book.
- Knit, sew, crochet, or cross-stitch something for you or your home.

- Enjoy the latest styles at your favorite boutique.
- Get the crayons out and buy yourself a coloring book. Then get to it.
- Play a hand of jacks or any other game that you loved as a child.
- Make popcorn and download or rent your favorite movie. Watch it either alone or with a friend.
- Meditate.

What activities will fill your day with more pleasure and FUN? Take any from above you want to make routine and add as many as you can think of that work with your lifestyle.

Practice the Four Rs: Relax, Restore, Regroup, Recharge

Learning to be gracious with yourself is like anything new you undertake. It takes **practice, patience,** and **persistence.** Naturally, pangs of guilt will start to surface as you're nicer to yourself. Pay no attention to them. It's par for the course!

CAMILLE PRESTON

Psychologist who runs a leadership training company, wife, mother

I love challenges and often seek them out. But this changed when I wanted to become a mom. This was not something I could do *my* way. I had difficulty getting pregnant. The doctors said to increase my chances, I should stop running, doing hot yoga, drinking coffee, wine, and eating *chocolate*! As if my struggle to conceive wasn't enough, they took away my coping mechanisms.

The journey was riddled with frustrations, a sense of failure, loneliness, embarrassment, and massive uncertainty—*would this ever happen?* My husband and I adopted a simple mantra that kept us focused—we wanted a happy and healthy baby. We let go of other things that didn't serve this mission;

people who didn't get it were put on hold. And after a while, I gave birth to my wonderful son.

Time Bandit

My time bandit is answering emails—I both love to stay connected and hate that there are always too many to answer. I try to end the day with no more than ten new messages in my inbox. They are usually the more complicated ones that demand more time. And I give myself periods during the day to respond to the others.

Time Enhancers

-   Create "me-time" moments. Know what makes you smile—things you love to do, people you enjoy doing them with.
-   Find NET time (things you enjoy that take No Extra Time).
-   Schedule your commute with a best friend and have gal-pal moments.
-   If you can't workout with a friend, the next best thing is a virtual workout. As you and a friend both run in different locations, connect with each other by phone.

Camille's Simple Pleasures

- writing
- yoga
- traveling
- making a great meal and experimenting with recipes

Camille's Best Advice

Celebrate the small steps as you change. Self-knowledge helps to create more energizing (vs. depleting) moments.

On the Power of Authenticity

Know who you are and what matters most. Speak your truth in a clear, engaging way. Too often we silence our voice and deny the world of our greatest gifts.

On the Power of Courage

I believe passion lies outside of our comfort zone. Life is nothing without adventure.

Who or what is your biggest time bandit? With awareness, you can turn this around and free yourself up for more joy in your life. What are three things you can do differently to have more time?

TRY THIS

Time Track: Actually keep tabs on how you spent your time today.

Write down in hourly increments what you did from the moment you got up in the morning until when you went to bed.

Become more aware about how you may be wasting time. Share your insights with a trusted friend.

Claim Your Passion

Now, what gets the blood racing in your veins? **What are you passionate about?** Think back to college, high school, even childhood—what were the things that excited you? Was it something that one of your friends was pursuing, but you were too afraid to try yourself? It could be anything—acting, scuba diving, running for office, giving a successful talk. The list goes on.

If you're having trouble thinking of something you'd like to bring into your life, try one of these exercises.

TRY THIS

Reflections of the Heart. Find a place where you feel comfortable, like a favorite chair in your living room or a quiet spot outdoors. Go there and close your eyes. Take a few deep breaths. Don't engage with the thoughts that are vying for your attention. Once you begin to relax, ask yourself, *What do I yearn to do that I haven't done?* Then listen to your heart answering the call. You will start to become aware of what you've been neglecting.

Sacred Writing. If inner reflection isn't generating any ideas about your passions, you may want to try stream of consciousness writing. Just grab paper and a pen, then write without thinking. Set a timer for five or ten minutes and see what you come up with. Don't stop; if you get stuck, focus on one word and write it over and over until you gain insight. Many people feel uncomfortable the first time they try this type of writing, but with practice, it can help you reach another level of awareness.

What do you yearn to do that you haven't done, something you are passionate about? What is getting in your way of doing it? Who could you ask for support to get started?

Now, visualize yourself doing it. What are you wearing? Who are you with? What impact are you having?

Write this in paragraph form and use "I" statements, as if it were happening now. Share what you have written with a trusted friend.

Actions to Nourish Your Soul

When you allow yourself experiences that nourish your soul, you become more efficient in doing the mundane things on your list. What actions will you commit to this month to pursue your passion?

When you bring a new activity into your life, do it one step at a time. If you were training for a marathon, you'd start with a mile and work your way up. The same is true for what you feel passionate about. If you want to paint, start by buying a set of oils, an easel, and some brushes. Experiment for a while and get back into the flow of the work, then when you feel ready, sign up for a class.

As you begin to make room for what truly excites you, expect some resistance, such as thinking *I'm being selfish* or *I've started too late and wasted too much time.* It's important that you don't listen to this mind-chatter. Just keep moving forward and pay attention to your inner guidance.

ANDREA ZINTZ

Mother of two young women,
wife, business owner

I am a driven person; I like to try new things and test my limits. I have an entrepreneurial leaning. I also have a tendency to take on too much. When my girls were young and I had a high-powered job, personal time became nonexistent. I felt fatigued and stressed; this accelerated when I left the corporation to start my own business. Then, I worked 24/7.

My husband is a source of inspiration. He has the ability to balance his teaching job with relaxing activities. One Sunday morning, he took the kids to see their grandparents and left me alone to regroup. I made a list of what restores me: singing, playing an instrument, hiking, skiing, golf, reading, massages, facials, movies, and time with friends. Then and there, I committed to bringing these things into my life again. I decided to hire someone to supervise the kids after school and brought a person in to do administrative tasks for my business. Taking these actions changed my life.

Time bandit

Travel is a challenge for me. When I'm on the road, I can't get to my favorite gym classes and don't have my usual routines. When I book travel, I make sure that my hotel has a gym. I pack my sneakers and workout clothes on trips.

Time enhancers

- Get some help with at-home activities if you can.
- Block out personal time on your calendar and honor it.
- Listen to your body, emotions, and sensations. They send messages about your self-care needs.

Andrea's Simple Pleasures

- singing in a chorus on Monday nights
- getting a facial or massage monthly
- playing golf, hiking, or exercising at the gym

Andrea's Best Advice

I still fall off the wagon and neglect my needs, so resolving to do it differently next time helps me to make better choices.

On the Power of Acknowledgment

I have a beautiful voice and a passion for music. After a short folk-singing career early on, I shifted to more lucrative work using other skills. But I sang in the car and to my children. Recently, I joined a local "Sweet Adelines" chorus. I love it.

How do we make room for those things that delight our soul, despite all our responsibilities?

Write down the actions that you will commit to doing this month to pursue your passion. Which ones will you do this week? What action or actions will you do today?

Practice

As with any muscle, your "inner" muscles—the ones that make you joyful—must be exercised regularly. Their upkeep is simple. **You need to make a conscious effort each day to think positively.** The reflections that follow will help you do that. Pick one and say it to yourself at different times during the day (on your commute, at lunch, etc.). Call a friend and share it with her. If it helps, write it down on notes to post around your home—put it on your computer, a mirror, or the refrigerator door. Write it in your journal.

There are enough reflections to last you two weeks if you choose to rotate them on a daily basis.

INNER UPKEEP

- I create new ways of playing and carve out the time to do so.
- I look at my surroundings as if I were seeing them for the first time.
- I allow the excitement of change to fill my life.
- I will not "react" to situations that cause me stress. Instead, I will observe what is going on.
- I take good care of myself by doing at least one thing just for me today.
- I use humor in all my affairs.
- I am exactly where I am supposed to be.
- I have enough time and energy to do what's needed today.
- I look at the people in my life as if I just met them.
- I make loving choices for myself.
- I let go of old habits and watch my life unfold. I stop rehashing worst-case scenarios.
- I see the potential in situations before me.
- My words serve to create kindness around me. I have compassion for myself. I am enough.

What reflection from above resonates with you the most?
Rewrite it here and make it your new mantra.

Create your own reflections. Write down three new ones and add them to your Inner Upkeep list.

After a week, write about the impact the reflections are having in your life here.

Quiet Time

We often get caught up in the rush of an activity, feeling as if there's never enough time to finish what we have to do. Thinking this way only creates greater frenzy and becomes a self-fulfilling prophecy. We end up **not having enough time**. It's useful to stop whatever you're doing when a "never-enough-time" attack comes on and **pause for a moment**. Breathe deeply. As you inhale—think "peace." As you exhale—think "tension gone."

TRY THIS

Permission to Rest. Sit in a comfortable chair and let your eyes close. Breathe deeply. As thoughts enter your mind, just note them. Continue breathing deeply. Now, listen to the sounds around you. Pinpoint the closest sound, the farthest sound. Keep listening. Tell yourself, *It's my time to relax.* Practice this each day for about three minutes.

We are so used to doing things for others that when we have a moment of free time, we may feel guilty and not take it for ourselves. **Give yourself permission to rest and enjoy your quiet time.**

TRY THIS

Pretend Laughter. After a long day or when you are in a bad mood, try laughing. Even if you can't find anything to laugh about, make yourself laugh—the louder the better. It feels silly at first; however, ultimately it will make you feel good. If tricking yourself into happiness isn't working for you, at least the image of how ridiculous you look laughing at nothing will bring a genuine smile to your face. Humor is the great equalizer, helping us to diffuse stress and allowing us to look on the bright side. Most of the things we think are crises really aren't, and **with a touch of humor, we can stop taking ourselves so seriously.**

TRY THIS

Carve Out "She" Time. Haven't gotten together with girlfriends lately? Don't wait any longer—initiate the calls and set it up. You'll feel renewed in the company of other women. In between face-to-face visits, send out caring emails and make phone calls.

TRY THIS

Schedule a Retreat. Whether going by yourself or with a friend, do the research and find that wonderful spot to renew yourself. You deserve it!

Tweak your schedule in your favor! Write out your daily schedule here and then look at it objectively. Make sure you set time for work, family, and social obligations, then list what's missing from your self-care routine (reading a book? calling a friend?) and rewrite your schedule with these items listed as TIME FOR YOU!

LINDA MORALES

Businesswoman, stepmom

A few years ago, I was working long hours with very little time for myself and family. I travel for work, and I would return from a trip and start the same routine again. When I'd have lunch with coworkers, we talked about work and vented. I felt stressed and very imbalanced.

My mother was diagnosed with breast cancer around Christmas, and my overwhelm skyrocketed—making it much worse. It was a busy time at work, so my sister took charge of mom's illness. But that didn't last long since her husband needed open-heart surgery. I knew I had to go to Medjugorje in Bosnia (a holy place of prayer) to ask for a miracle for my mother and brother-in-law. When I was away, **I began to reflect on my own life.** Did I want to continue living this unhealthy lifestyle? The answer was clearly no. In looking back, my mother's illness was a catalyst for taking better care of myself.

Time Bandit

Overscheduling myself... On my last birthday, I had four fun commitments, but I was exhausted when it was over. I had not done my laundry, my place was a mess, and I was exhausted. I allowed myself to stay home the following day, sleep a few extra hours, and work from home in my pajamas.

Time Enhancers

-   Get to work on time, not earlier. Use the extra hour to get to the gym or take time to reflect or take a walk.
-   Take an hour for lunch—decompress, window shop, listen to music.
-   On weekends, have sacred family time.
-   Learn something new—take a class.
-   Give up guilt!

Linda's Simple Pleasures

-   At age fifty-two, I learned to ride a bike—I love it!
-   taking Photoshop and Italian classes
-   meditating on the beach

On the Power of Risk

What better example of overcoming risk than learning how to ride a bike in your fifties! The desire to learn was greater than my fear, and I took one step at a time. Thank goodness for YouTube! **When going downhill, you have to let go completely and allow gravity, energy, wind, and the universe to bring you down and lift you up again!**

Linda's Best Advice

When I was "wired," I had to admit that I didn't have the solutions, but others did. I began to ask for help and take suggestions. **Reach out for support.**

Who makes up your support system? If a challenge came up today, who could you reach out to for help?

Conclusion

Take the list below of "sparkle sustainers" and make a copy of it. Place it where you can see it at home and at the office. Glance at these simple sayings throughout the day and be sure to read the whole list when you are feeling particularly stretched. The practical wisdom here is applicable to most situations:

- Speak out on issues you feel passionate about.
- Don't procrastinate; just do it!
- When you feel yourself tensing up, breathe deeply.
- What you can change, change. What you can't, leave it alone—let go!
- When you make a mistake, don't dwell on it. Move on—next!
- When you receive criticism, take what fits and leave the rest.
- When you are about to criticize someone, *stop*. Look at what's bothering you.
- Before you act in a way you will regret—*think*.

- Don't force solutions—answers will evolve in their proper time.
- When disputes arise, look for the common ground—it's there.
- Offer praise like it is going out of style.

In this book, you have been given the tools to carve out and maintain time for you. Now use them to bring more joy into your life. Join the many women who are chanting a new mantra:

Time for **me**.

Time for Me Takeaways

Be More, Not Do More
Incorporate **resting, reflecting,** and **spending time with yourself** into your daily routine. Commit to new actions you intend to take.

Say No and Let Go of Guilt
What are some of the things you don't want to do anymore? Make a point to say no the next time you are asked to do one of them. If you need to, call a friend for support.

Don't Take It Personally
Come up with statements you can tell yourself the next time you are criticized and feel like reacting. Remember—it probably has nothing to do with you!

Remain Flexible
Recognize when you're becoming rigid or a bit compulsive because you're attempting to do something *exactly* right. **Perfectionism robs you of living joyously.**

You're on your way to making more TIME for YOU! As a result of what you've learned in this book, pick one of your goals that feels most important at the moment. How will you move forward today, taking a step toward achieving it? Good luck!

Acknowledgments

Special thanks to Deb Werksman for her vision and introduction to Mac Anderson—a luminary in his own right. To my original editor, Alice Patenaude, and my intern, Tess Mangiardi, for their dedication to creating an important book. To Meg Gibbons, Sarah Otterness, and Cailin Loesch for this new edition and journal. To the Turkey Land Cove Foundation for providing a retreat house, where I put the final touches on the manuscript. To Sarah Cooke, who kept us on the right track. And to Becky Post, for her support.

Most importantly, to you, the women out in the trenches every day, trying to do it all—may you find time for yourself. That is my deepest desire.

About the Author

Helene Lerner is the founder of WomenWorking.com. As an empowerment expert, she is a prolific author, independent public television host, Emmy award–winning executive producer, and workplace consultant. An influencer in social media, Helene has a following of over 19 million people.

Her career began as a teacher in the New York City public school system. Using her innate business instincts, she later pursued sales and marketing assignments during the 1980s, working her way up through the management ranks of the *New York Times*. She is currently the CEO of Creative Expansions, Inc., a multimedia company whose mission is to empower women and girls. She advises corporations on leadership and diversity issues.

A member of Phi Beta Kappa, Helene holds an MBA from Pace

University and a Master's in Education from City College in New York City, where she currently resides.

Her website, WomenWorking.com, is one of the premier websites for career women. It offers strategies on leadership, advancement, and navigating work/life, as well as a multimedia blog with posts from career coaches.

womenworking.com   @womenworking

@womenworking   WomenWorking group

TIME FOR ME

NOTES